## MAKE MONEY FROM HOME WITH PRINT ON DEMAND PRODUCTS MERCH BY AMAZON & KINDLE DIRECT PUBLISHING

## ASHLEY L SCHMITT

AshSchmitt.com

Mobile Military Spouse

ISBN: 9798654717719

Copyright © 2020

Ashley L Schmitt

Ashschmitt.com

# Introduction

11 moves in 20 years. That's my story. A typical military spouse story. A story filled with joy and challenges, but it's a story about being on the move and ever trying to find your place in the world.

A story of packing up all of your belongs only to unpack them a few weeks later. Then, just when you find a routine and are getting settled (not to mention finding that other shoe you've been looking for, *for the past year*, in a box that was forgotten in a closet), you have to start figuring out how to pack up your life to move again. Does any of that sound familiar?

Or how about knowing you are going to move in two months, so you start to make creative dinners from what you have left in your pantry. My kids may not be excited about the frozen broccoli I found in the back of the freezer, but the box of emergency Mac N Cheese is a winner.

Ahh moving….. and what about finding a job if you want one? That can be tough with different states requiring different certifications or maybe you are only at that base for a few months. Well, that makes finding a job pointless.

BUT…. You want a little spending cash or just a way to make some money and contribute. I know I did.

I'm a smart, intelligent woman. While I love to cook, raise my children, and do all the several thousand tasks a homemaker does…. I wanted something for me.

Enter Print on Demand or POD as it is affectionately known. It has been my passion for over 5 years and in that time, I have created and published more than 2000 books, and over 1000 T-shirt designs.

And do you want to know the best part? I did this without a garage full of books or shirts, AND it was a completely FREE business to start.

Yes, let me repeat that. This business is completely FREE to start. Now, the steps are easy and really anyone can start and succeed at this business, but it does take WORK. It is not a get rich quick scheme, it is a long-term business that you can start and grow completely for FREE in your spare time. (While it is true you CAN start for free there are a few great and inexpensive tools that make the process much easier.)

In this guide, I'll reveal

- What an amazing opportunity POD is
- Where to go to get started
- How to get started
- How to stand out and get your products selling

Just so you know who I am and can get to know me better there is a link below with a video introduction about me, my publishing career, and why I love POD!

Use the link below or scan the QR code with your smartphone camera. And while you are there subscribe to my YouTube Channel for weekly tips!

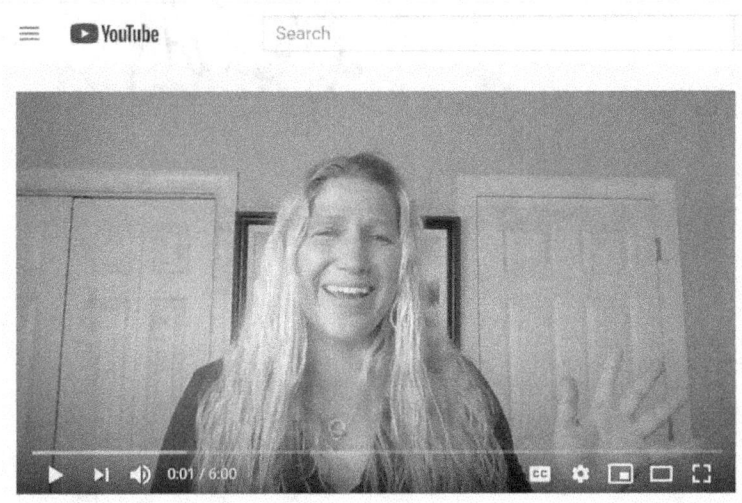

https://youtu.be/WwHacG-jTno

# YES, you can make money from publishing books.

Here's my earnings for December 2019.

I had been publishing fiction and non-fiction books since 2015. I loved writing but with 4 young children to care for I was finding it harder to find the amount of time I needed to really focus on my writing. Instead of being fun, it had become a chore. I knew I wanted to continue publishing (it was the perfect business, one I started for free, could work whenever I wanted, and got a passive income from) so in January 2019, I decided to shift my focus to workbooks, journals, and planners. I could do research and quickly turn it into a product. Instead of working on a book for months, I could publish something in a day to a week, depending on the project. It was perfect! Less than a year later, I had a fabulous December. These results are not magic or a get rich quick scheme. They were the result of **consistent effort over time** and a willingness to adjust and refocus on the things that were working. You can succeed too! It just requires the determination to keep going.

# Contents

- So, What Is POD?..................................................................8
- How Do I Get Started?.........................................................10
- Ways To Create And Publish Books Using Kindle Direct Publishing (KDP) ...............................................................11
- Novels, Short Reads, and Non-Fiction (Content Books).. 13
- Journals & Planners (Low Content Books) ......................16
- Types of Low Content Books ..............................................17
- Designing your book ............................................................19
- Uploading Your Book...........................................................24
- Selling T-Shirts and Other Merchandise on Amazon the Merch By Amazon Program...............................................28
- Trademark Search ................................................................32
- Selling/Marketing .................................................................33
- Conclusion ............................................................................36

Nope not these cute pea pods!

# So, What Is POD?

Basically, is a the most amazing business opportunity out there. It is a fabulous way to build a business and make money from the comfort of your own home, couch, bed, or wherever. All you need is an internet connection and a computer or laptop. (Some of it can actually be done with your smartphone, but a computer is easier in some cases.)

I want to repeat that POD isn't a scam, and it isn't easy money but it is a business opportunity I have come to love with my military lifestyle that can and DOES get uprooted all the time. I can take it with me anywhere I go.

POD, print on demand, is pretty much what it sounds like. Products that are printed on demand. A customer orders the product off the internet (in this book we'll talk mostly about Amazon since it is the biggest and easiest to start opportunity out there) and it is "printed" and shipped to the customer.

What kind of products? There are thousands but since we are focusing on Amazon we are talking about books, T-shirts, tank tops, long sleeve shirts, raglans shirts, sweatshirts, Popsockets, and a few other items. Amazon will continue to add "merch" or merchandise, but generally speaking, T-shirts and books are the biggest sellers.

The concept is you create the book (interior and cover) or the design that will go on the T-shirt. You upload your electronic files on to Amazon's creator websites, add a description, input a sales price, and submit.

Yep, that's it! You don't have to do ANYTHING else. Your product (after it passes a review process to make sure it is in the right format and that you are not uploading copywritten material—no Disney, Marvel, or branded stuff) appears on Amazon for anyone to purchase. Amazon handles everything. You don't have to print a T-shirt, book, or send anything to a customer. No returns or dealing with customer service. Amazon does it all!

Even better than not having to haul around inventory or worry if you can sell it all before you move, your product is listed as an Amazon Prime product. If you have Amazon Prime, you know the power of that. How many times have you only bought an item because it was Amazon Prime and didn't have to pay for shipping? Or you paid an extra dollar for the Amazon Prime item because you NEEDED it in 2 days!

If you aren't a Prime member, this behavior might not make sense, but know that the majority of shoppers on Amazon prefer Prime items. So, an Amazon Prime listing is a big deal!

# How Do I Get Started?

Amazon's two main platforms are Kindle Direct Publishing and Merch By Amazon.

Kindle Direct Publishing or KDP is where you can publish ebooks and paperback books. And while you CAN write "The Great American Novel" or your own version of Harry Potter, you don't have to limit yourself to novels. We'll talk about this more later in the book, but don't put KDP out of your head because you think you can't write. This is A HUGE OPPORTUNITY and so much more than writing a novel. But you can do that too. I have quite a few of those as well.

 KDP is a platform that you can sign up for and get started right away. Go to https://kdp.amazon.com

Merch By Amazon is Amazon's merchandise platform. Currently, it includes apparel like T-shirts, tank tops, v-necks, sweatshirts, long-sleeved shirts, raglans, hoodies, zipper sweatshirts, and Popsockets. More items will be added as Amazon decides what will sell the best.

Merch By Amazon is currently allowing people to apply and not everyone is able to get an account. But definitely try to get an account. Go to https://merch.amazon.com/ to apply for an account.

# Ways To Create And Publish Books Using Kindle Direct Publishing (KDP)

KDP is a fantastic opportunity if you can think beyond a novel. If writing is your passion, then don't let me stop you from carrying out that dream. I started down that road, am still on that road, AND expanded my possibilities of what I could do with ebooks and printed books.

Here are just a few ideas:

- Novels
- Short reads
- Non-fiction topics
- Memoirs
- Children's chapter books
- Children's books
- Very Young Children's Books
- Joke books
- Puzzle books
- Coloring books
- Journals
- Calendars
- Planners
- Notebooks
- Composition books
- Travel Journals
- Event books

There is a massive opportunity out there to provide more types of books than you can possibly imagine at this point. I know when I started, I could barely think of 10 types of books. Now, I could come up with a list of 1000 without a problem. One of the best ways I have come up with winning book ideas is to think about a problem I am having and then come up with a book that will solve that problem.

Now, there are two types of books you can sell on KDP; ebooks and paperback books. Depending on the purpose of the book, it could be one, or the other, or both. For example, a novel can be an ebook or a paperback, while a journal or planner can only be a printed book. Just imagine if you purchased an ebook journal and all it had was blank lines on a kindle screen. You can't write on it, so it would be useless! You would be unhappy. So, when making a book think about how the end customer would use it, and that will tell you what kind of book you can make.

# Novels, Short Reads, and Non-Fiction (Content Books)

**Novels:** I'm not sure novels need much introduction or explanation, but novels tend to be categorized as fiction, but there are genres of novels like memoirs or based on true stories that are non-fiction. The heart of a novel is that it tells a story. Novels tend to be classified by story length or word count.

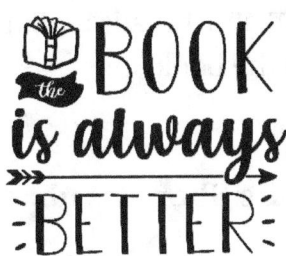

**Novel:** 40,000 words or over

**Novella:** 17,500 to 39,999 words

**Novelette:** 7,500 to 17,499 words

**Short story:** under 7,500 words

Don't forget about Children's Books. Chapter books are very popular and cover age appropriate topics. The length depends on the child's age. Also, picture or drawings are common for early readers.

Very early readers or young children tend to enjoy books with colorful pictures and shorter, simple stories.

Whatever genre, adult or children, novel or children's books you are interested in writing, do your research. Read stories within that genre, browse bookstores, and check out what is selling on Amazon.

**Short Reads:** Amazon has its own category of books for it's kindle e-readers. They are called short reads and are defined by the average amount of time it takes a person to read the book.

**Kindle Short Reads**

15 minutes (1-11 pages)

30 minutes (12-21 pages)

45 minutes (22-32 pages)

One hour (33-43 pages)

90 minutes (44-64 pages)

Two hours or more (65-100 pages)

If you want to start out with content books, Short Reads might be a great place to start. A 40,000+ word novel might seem daunting, but a 6-11 page short story, might be a great first step.

Again, do some research to see what is on Amazon and what is selling. Though, if it is your first try at writing a story, you should write about something you are familiar with. Keep in mind, if is your first story, it will probably be your worst (it **is** your first attempt, so give yourself a break) AND it probably won't sell a million copies and make you a millionaire. It could, but the likelihood of that happening is very small. Think of your first few short reads as learning experiences. Enjoy the creative process of making something and then seeing it up on Amazon!

**Non-Fiction:** Non-fiction is a great place to start. Know a useful skill? Are you an expert at something? Does everyone ask you to show them how to do something? Write a book about that! This book is a non-fiction book with an overview of many of the things I have learned over the past 5 years publishing books and creating other print on demand products.

Non-fiction topics are endless and depending on what you choose to write about the book could be a longer or shorter book. A great way to start is to think about a topic you know a lot about and pick the 5 or 10 most important things about that topic. Create a Top 5 or Top 10 Things You Need to Know About ____ book. You can write an introduction and then each of the 5 or 10 things could be a chapter. The last chapter is the conclusion.

Non-fiction books can also be short reads. Do you make the BEST chocolate chip cookies on the planet? Do you cook a to-die-for rack of ribs? Detail your process and put it in a "how-to" book for readers. A short book is good in this case. No one wants to read a 100-page book about 1 recipe for cookies. (I love cookies, but 100 pages is way too much. Just tell me how to make them so I can EAT them!)

# Journals & Planners (Low Content Books)
## - This is where I suggest you start -

What is a Low Content Book? It's really a made-up term, but it includes books that have no to a small amount of words. Not novels, or short reads, or non-fiction. Think journals (no words, just lines), planners (some words and dates), gratitude journals, prompt books, etc. Simple books but VERY useful. I love notebooks. I collect them. I adore the many fun colorful covers and all my scattered thoughts and notes inside.

The reason I suggest you start with low content books is because they are the easiest to start with. Writing a 50,000-word novel is doable, but it takes a lot more time and effort than creating a journal or planner. The first goal when you start this business is to get something published.

Let me repeat that the 1st goal is TO GET SOMETHING PUBLISHED. Don't over think it. Don't make it hard on yourself. And don't worry if it isn't great. I'll be honest, completely honest, your first book no matter how long you spend will probably be your worst. So, just get it over with. Make something that is just okay and publish it. The first 10 or so journals you make will just be learning the process. Don't' spend a ton of time; it isn't worth it.

Your first project should be something for yourself. Create a lined notebook with a fun cover that you like. Then, you can buy your own product and test it out. If you are the only purchaser of that book, that's okay. You'll make it, use it, and learn the process. That's a win!

And believe me, when your book gets delivered to your house and you open the package you will be thrilled! Most exciting thing ever!

# Types of Low Content Books

There are an endless amount and kinds of low content books. We've already mentioned a few and there are many others, such as:

- Joke books
- Puzzle books
- Coloring books
- Journals
- Calendars
- Planners
- Notebooks
- Composition books
- Travel journals
- Event books
- Workbooks
- Prompt books
- Logbooks
- Guest books
- Vision boards
- Camping journals
- Medical journals/logs
- Pet logs
- Diet/Food trackers

The books above are just a few of the kinds of books you can create, but let's look at how you can create hundreds of books by just focusing on one kind of book. Let's take a guest book. A guest book typically includes lines to write someone's name, the date, and notes or comments. Look on Amazon or find a guest logbook at a bookstore. You'll see that the interior is very simple. Once you have created an interior you can make hundreds of kinds of books by adjusting the interior and creating several types of covers.

For example, B&B's need guestbooks and there are B&Bs all over the world with different themes such as country, city, western, forest, or mountains. You could create skiing guestbooks for Colorado B&Bs or Western themed guestbooks for Dude Ranches in Texas. There are a million other combinations.

The best way to succeed is to focus on niches. A B&B next to the ocean will want an ocean scene on the cover and a few seashell clipart pictures or icons in the corners of the interior.

There are also event guestbooks like birthday parties, Halloween parties, weddings, or baby showers. Just use your imagination to think of all the other types of guest books you can create.

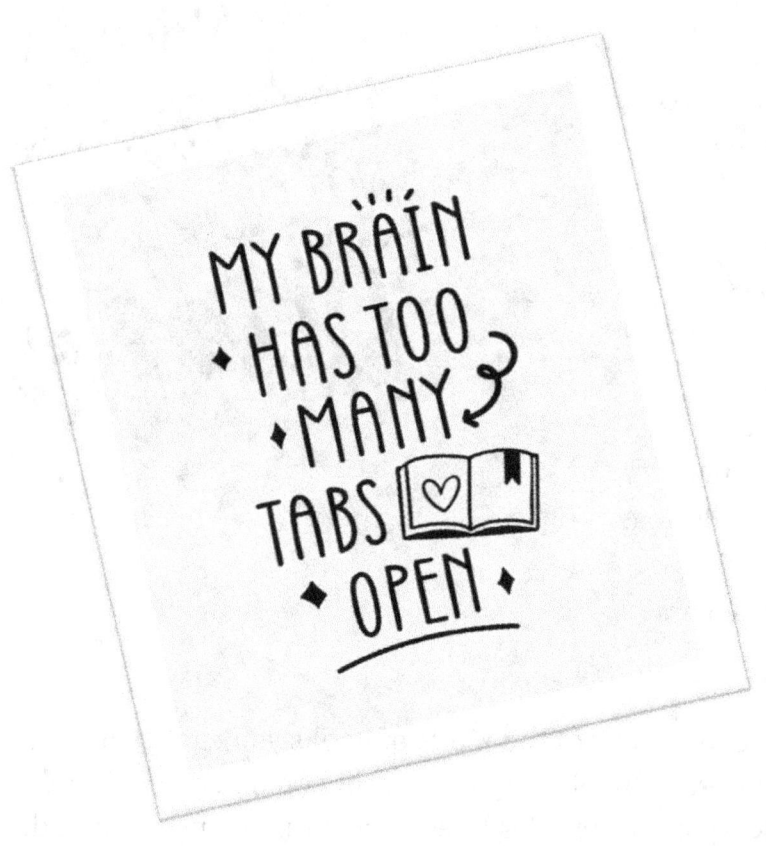

# Designing your book

Once you've decided on what type of book to create (and I suggest you start with a simple blank lined notebook for yourself) you need to consider what software you want to design it with. No matter what type of book you create, paperback or ebook, you will need to create two files; 1) the interior 2) the cover.

Amazon's KDP platform has a good help center with lots of videos located at

https://kdp.amazon.com/en_US/help

I've found the information helpful, but sometimes a bit confusing. In another section, I have a video that walks through the process of uploading a book. It will be a simple lined journal, but as I said your first goal is to get something published.

So how do I create an interior and cover? And what software can I design it with?

Let's start with software. There are several free and paid options. Since this book is aimed at military spouses, I suggest using Microsoft products. Microsoft Word and PowerPoint are what I use exclusively at this point. The reason I recommend these for military spouses is that you are eligible for Microsoft's Home Use Program. Your spouse can use their military email address to sign up for a reduced license for Microsoft 365. (If you already have an older version of Word or PowerPoint those will work.)

Check it out at https://www.microsoft.com/en-us/home-use-program

There are other options, and I'll talk about them below.

## Word

Word is a fantastic program for creating ebook or paperback interiors for content type books (such as novels, non-fiction, and short reads). This book was created in a Word document. You can create low content books such as journals and planners using Word, but I wouldn't recommend it. Word functions best for documents that contain paragraphs of information.

If you want to create ebook interiors using Word, KDP will accept Word document .docx files for upload and convert the file to a .mobi file (.mobi is the file format used on kindle e-readers). It's fairly simple to just upload the .docx file and then you are able to preview what the ebook version would look like.

For paperbacks, you will need to make sure you have the correct size pages. If you want to create a 6 x 9 inch book then you will need to make sure the Word doc page size is 6 x 9 inches.

KDP provides word document templates. Search KDP Help for paperback templates or go to:

https://kdp.amazon.com/en_US/help/topic/G201834230

## PowerPoint

I love to create workbooks and other low content books. PowerPoint is my favorite program to create books. I have tried almost every product out there (free and paid) and PowerPoint is still my favorite program for interiors AND covers. There are so many reasons but the 3 main reasons I love PowerPoint are:

1) Once I understood templates and how to set up my books, I NEVER got a book rejected for sizing or format problems. (You have no idea how infuriating it can be to spend HOURS trying to figure out why your book is showing errors or getting rejected for a sizing issue.) PowerPoint gives me full control on sizing my document and the set up. Many paid cover or interior creators might be "easy," but I have always had trouble with saving, sizing problems, and corrupted files.
2) PowerPoint is a powerful program with a lot of built in features that make creating books and interiors easy.
3) I can create Macros programs. I admit this one is an advanced reason, but I did a bit of research and learned to code a few automated routines to make creating books easier and faster. If you decide to take my KDP Publishing Bootcamp course, I include some of my favorite Macros programs, and show you how to use them. (No coding necessary, just hit run.) I also include interior and cover templates!

You can check out KDP Publishing Bootcamp Course at: www.ashschmitt.com

(Or if you just want 365+ Low Content Book ideas go to www.ashschmitt.com and sign up for my superstar VIP list!)

## Google Docs & Google Slides

Google Docs and Google Slides are similar to Word and PowerPoint. They are free options, and I know many people who use them to create their books. Google Docs is great for content book interiors. Google Slides can be used for low content book interiors and covers.

## Apple Pages & Keynote

If you are a Mac user then you can use Apple Pages as your word processing program and Keynote for low content interiors as well as creating covers. I am a PC user, so I am not as familiar with these programs, but I have friends who love to use them.

## Canva

Canva is an online solution that is free. There is a paid, pro version, but I have never needed the pro version. The great thing about Canva is you can create covers and low content interiors. Also, any of the graphics that say FREE you can use for commercial use projects. So, if it is FREE you are able to use it on or in your books. Check it out at https://www.canva.com/ Sign up and create a free account. This is one of the software programs I started with and still use occasionally. It is a great free way to start your publishing business.

## Affinity Products

Affinity has a line of high-quality graphic design products. Affinity Publisher is well suited to design covers and low content book interiors. It is a quality product with a one-time fee. Many other similar products are monthly/yearly subscription products. The only negative to Affinity Publisher is there is a bit of a learning curve. Check out Affinity Publisher here: https://affinity.serif.com/en-us/

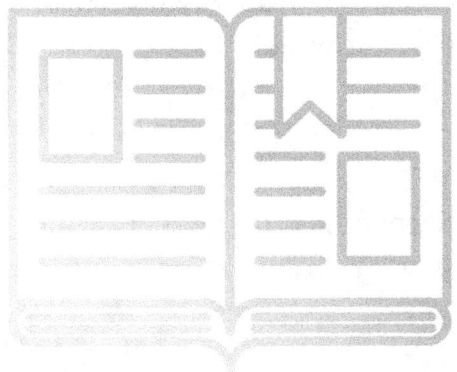

# Graphics & Fonts

## Graphics

There are many places to get free graphics and paid graphics for your books' interiors and covers. The MOST IMPORTANT PART is to make sure you can use them for commercial use. You need commercial use rights AND you need to make sure you can use them for printed materials and books.

Don't take a short cut on this. If you are using free or paid graphics, you must read the license that comes with what you plan to use. Many sites want you to change the graphic or add other elements. Some want you to only sell a certain amount with that product on it before you need to buy another license. You must READ the rules. If you have questions, email the site and ask.

Beware of sites that offer free graphics. There are some very reputable sites, but if you decide to download items, make sure to change the imagine AND do a Google reverse image search. If you don't know how to do this just Google "Google reverse image search."

The purpose of the reverse image search is to make sure someone didn't download the image from a paid site and then upload to a free site. If this is the case, don't use that image. Your books can be taken down and Amazon can decide to close your account. So, be careful and always read license rules.

We will talk about Merch By Amazon next and you can use the resources listed below for your t-shirt designs, BUT again you must read the license rules. Books and t-shirts are different. Many graphics sites will be fine with your use of graphics on books but will not be okay with use on t-shirts or other items.

Here are a few graphics resources. These are my favorites. If you subscribe to their email lists, they offer freebies of the day or week.

 Depositphotos https://depositphotos.com/

 VectorStock https://www.vectorstock.com/

 Creative Fabrica https://www.creativefabrica.com/ref/237976/ (This link is an affiliate link. I may make a small commission, but it won't cost you anything)

![theHungryJpeg logo] theHungryJpeg  https://thehungryjpeg.com/

There are many other graphic sites online, you just need to look around. Be sure to read the license agreements. I tend to use paid for resources instead of free resources. The paid resources really make your books stand out from the crowd. (The weekly freebies are great "free" resources but have the high-quality look you want. So, check those out.)

## Fonts

Fonts can really make the difference in printed books. Font type won't matter in ebooks since Amazon/the ereader controls that, but spending some time or money getting the right font for a project is well worth the effort.

When I first started, I purchased a set of 100 fonts from HungryJpeg for $19. They are always having a sale, and I still download their free weekly font if I like it. Now, I have too many ☺

Good quality fonts will make your work stand out and give your products a professional look.

My favorite places to get fonts are:

Creative Fabrica https://www.creativefabrica.com/ref/237976/ (This link is an affiliate link. I may make a small commission, but it won't cost you anything)

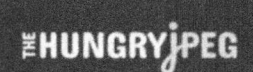 theHungryJpeg  https://thehungryjpeg.com/

# Uploading Your Book

To upload your book, you'll need your cover and interior finished. Once you have those two items you can upload and get your book on its way to being published.

But how exactly do I do that?

Well, I decided that trying to explain how to upload a book in words would be difficult. Instead, I've created a private video for you on my YouTube channel demonstrating how to upload a journal with lots of tips and trick included. (Remember start with something simple for your first book. Blank lined journals are a great first project.)

You'll need the link below or scan the QR code with your smartphone camera to be taken directly to the video. While you are on my YouTube channel you should subscribe!

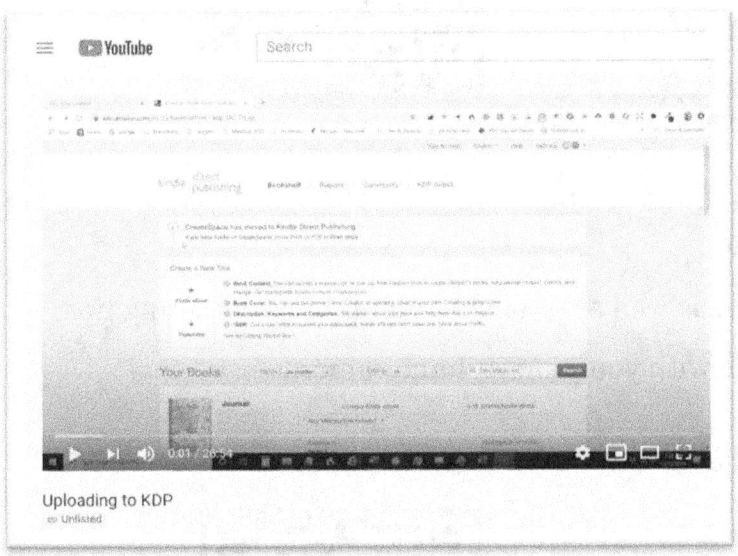

http://youtu.be/I6V4k67QCjo?hd=1

## Bonus Uploading/ Formatting Videos from Kindle Direct Publishing

Amazon provides many resources through their own webinar series. Check out the following pages with four of their introductory videos.

Take a tour of the KDP website and learn about requirements and resources for book formatting.

Use the link below or scan the QR code with your smartphone camera.

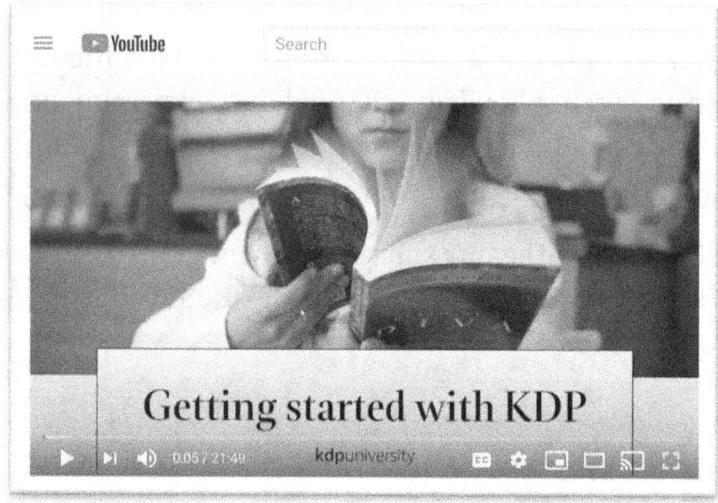

https://www.youtube.com/watch?v=cF0VkkJY2fM

Here's an overview of the KDP website, as well as publishing tools and marketing tips. Use the link below or scan the QR code with your smartphone camera.

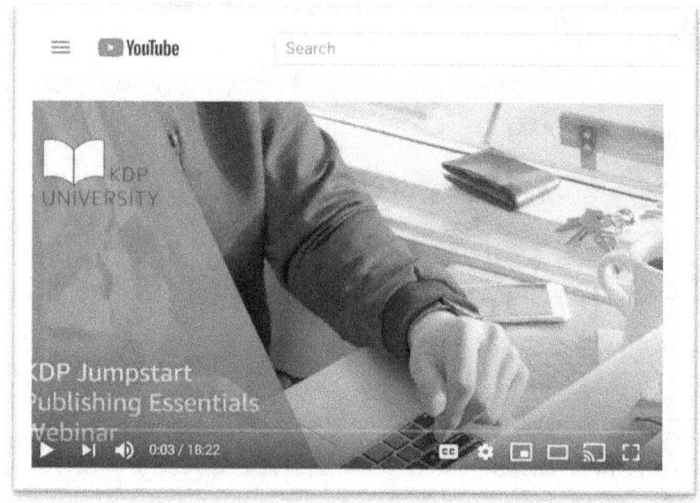

https://www.youtube.com/watch?v=BpqR4W0rjj0

This video will teach you industry terms and how to turn a completed manuscript into a formatted file.

Use the link below or scan the QR code with your smartphone camera.

https://www.youtube.com/watch?v=fWbaETodLFs

A great video to learn about cover formatting, branding principles, and the top 10 cover best practices.

Use the link below or scan the QR code with your smartphone camera.

https://www.youtube.com/watch?v=u6zRIXw19Jo

# Selling T-Shirts and Other Merchandise on Amazon the Merch By Amazon Program

## Applying for an Account

Go to https://merch.amazon.com/ to apply for an account.

Not everyone who applies gets accepted. Amazon is continually changing the rules on this program and no one outside of Amazon really knows what the magic key to acceptance is. Sometimes it seems everyone gets in and other times very few. If you get accepted on your first try, great. If not, rethink what you put on your application. Maybe add more information or less depending on what you tried before. You must use a different email address to try to reapply.

Once you have an account, you can start designing and uploading.

# Got An Account. Now What?

Congrats! You don't need to be a graphic designer to make some great selling t-shirts. It wouldn't hurt to have a background in design, but I know hundreds of successful Merch sellers that can't draw a stick figure. And when they started, they had no idea how to design. But they learned and you can too.

There are many programs to create a design for Merch By Amazon. It all depends on what programs you know and if you want to use a PC, Mac, your smartphone, or an online designer. The main thing to know is that you will need a program that can create a 4500 x 5400 pixel design with a transparent background PNG file.

Programs to check out are.

 Merch Informer Designer – https://merchinformer.com/901.html

The designer is part of Merch Informer. Use the **discount code ashley20** and get 20% off!

(This link is an affiliate link. I may get a commission but it doesn't cost you anything.)

 Photoshop - https://www.adobe.com/products/photoshop.html

 Affinity Designer - https://affinity.serif.com/en-us/designer/

 Over App (For Apple & Andriod) - Download the App from your app store. There is a free version and a pro version. Start with the free version to see if it is for you. I know a lot of people who upload the app to their phone and design all the time. Standing in line? Well, then you have time to design a t-shirt or two.

Chris Green has a great playlist on YouTube that goes through designing on the Over App.

Use the link below or scan the QR code with your smartphone camera.

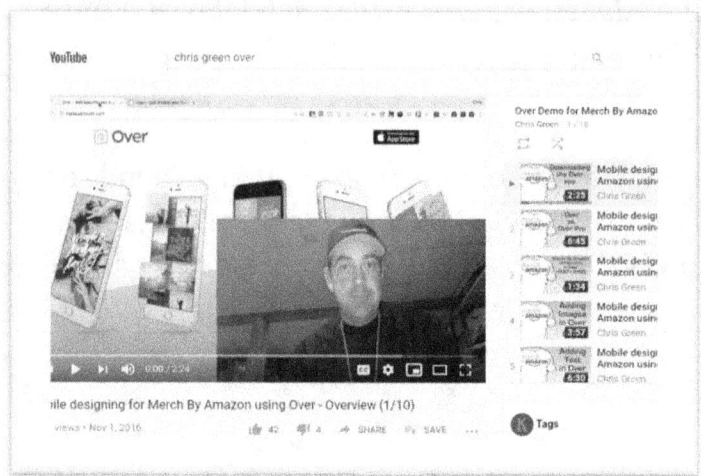

https://www.youtube.com/watch?v=I41EaaTwzP8&list=PLGy1_FmEQT1Kf8KjEZ0Pl0OP2GTNzw7pn

## Upload to Merch By Amazon

I have over 1000 T-shirts on Merch By Amazon but I tend to focus on KDP. I LOVE KDP & writing books, creating printables, digital planners, and workbooks. But here is quick video showing you how to upload a design to Merch By Amazon.

Use the link below or scan the QR code with your smartphone camera.

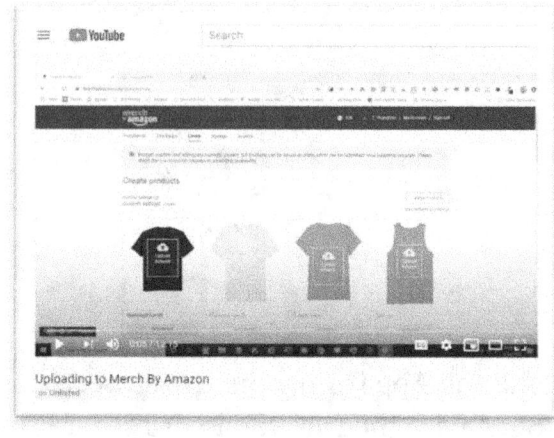

https://youtu.be/hMEaYCIGxQ4

## Graphics for Merch By Amazon

You actually don't need graphics. Many people are very successful without using graphics at all. They design t shirt with just text with funny sayings or something that appeals to a certain group of people. Starting with text is a good way to begin. Though, adding a graphic does increase the likelihood it will catch a buyer's interest when they are scrolling through.

I like to use Creative Fabrica since they have very clear rules on how their graphics can be used on POD items.

 Creative Fabrica https://www.creativefabrica.com/ref/237976/

Another great option is Merch Informer. This paid tool has (at the time of this writing) over 3000 graphics you can use on your POD shirts and merchandise. Also, it is a fantastic tool for doing research on what is selling, creating your designs, and has tools to make listing your designs so much easier.

Merch Informer https://merchinformer.com/901.html

Use the **discount code ashley20** and get 20% off!


## Merch Informer

Merch Informer is pretty much the gold standard in POD shirt design. You can do research, design, and use the uploader to make uploads easier. Below is another video that will walk you through what the program is and can do.

Use the link below or scan the QR code with your smartphone camera.

https://youtu.be/t8QNl-bcz08


(Creative Fabrica & Merch Informer are affiliate links. I may get a commission, but it doesn't cost you anything.)

# Trademark Search

The #1 most important thing to understand is you cannot use trademarked designs, items, characters, or wording in your books or t-shirt designs. While some trademarks might be obvious like Marvel comics or Disney Princesses, others may not be as obvious.

Here's my legal disclaimer. I am not a lawyer, so if you have questions, please consult a lawyer, but I can give you some basic guidance so you can do your own research. If you are publishing in the US, (which is currently the biggest market) you need to get familiar with the United States Patent and Trademark Office's Trademark Electronic Search System (TESS). TESS allows you to research the US Patent Office's for pending, current, and expired word trademarks.

TESS http://tmsearch.uspto.gov/bin/gate.exe?f=tess&state=4802:16xtyo.1.1

Check out the link and do your own research. Books and t-shirts (apparel) are indifferent categories so you need to search for trademarks for books in the book category and trademarks for t-shirts in the apparel category.

It might be slightly confusing at first. But don't discount my advice. You should do research into this area and do several searches on TESS. Once you figure out how to navigate the system, it starts to make sense. But ignoring my advice and blindly publishing things will get your account suspended or closed.

You don't need to be an expert but DO spend some time researching.

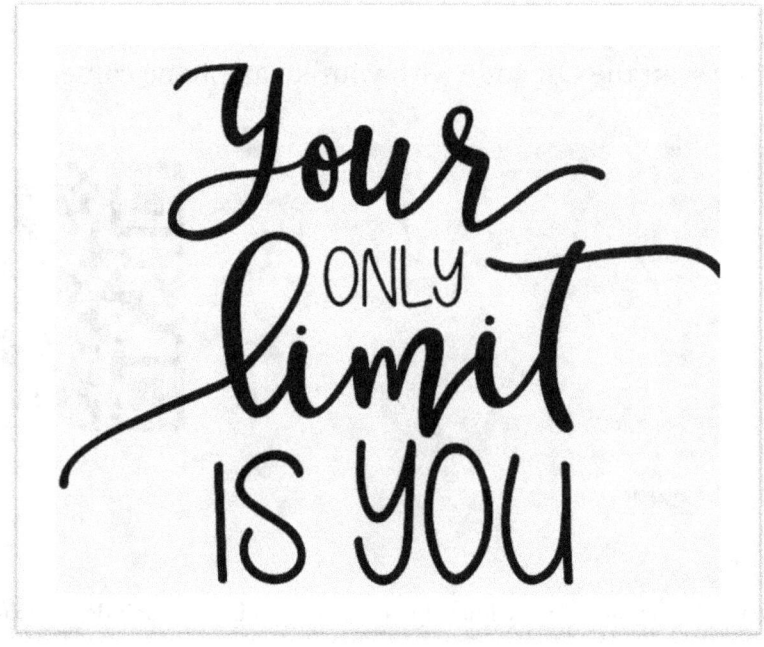

# Selling/Marketing

The fantastic thing about publishing books and t-shirts on Amazon is that you can just publish and forget about it. You don't have to do customer support, fill orders, make things, buy a bunch of items and store them in your garage, or anything like that.

BUT.... If you think you can make the design, toss it up online, and it will magically sell and make you a million dollars you are dreaming. (Or the luckiest person on earth and if so congrats!) This IS a business and any business requires work.

In the video about uploading, I talked about the importance of keywords. Doing research in what keywords a person might use to search for your book is very important. If you choose good keywords and your book resonates with your audience, then you have a very good chance of selling your product organically. (Meaning people find your product by searching and you don't have to do any additional marketing.)

That sounds great right? And yes, it can be, but you will get better results if you do a little marketing. There are a ton of ways to market.

A simple one that is free, is to create books or designs around a certain niche. Start a Facebook group, offer quotes or topics of discussion that your audience would find valuable. Sprinkle in advertisement of your products after you've given them valuable information. As you get to know your audience you can ask them what products they want and you can make those products for them

You can tell your family and friends about your products. You can make product specifically for family and friends.

Paid advertising is an option, too. I would suggest starting with Amazon Advertising.

Amazon Advertising is Amazon's advertising systems within the Amazon site. If you've been on Amazon you've already seen a bunch of sponsored Ads.

Advertising on Amazon is a more advance topic, if you choose to do this type of paid advertising, make sure you have several products uploaded. (Remember your first products probably won't be your best, so don't waste money advertising them until you really understand what you are doing.)

My advice for the newbie:

1) Create several products.
2) Research and learn about keywords and phrases.
3) Use free advertising methods like telling friends and family about your books. A few sales are always a boost to the ego.
4) Once you have a few items selling organically (without paid ads) think about moving onto more advanced advertising methods.

Moving into more advance marketing strategies too early can be a waste of time and expensive. In the beginning you are just learning. Let yourself learn. It can be tempting to make 5 or 10 items and then wonder why you aren't making thousands of dollars. The truth is your books or designs, might just not be that good or interesting yet. Spending marketing money or a ton of time isn't worth it until you learn your craft.

Remember Algebra? (Maybe you try hard to forget.) But you probably didn't go to class the first day and know it all. It took time and effort to learn. The great thing about POD is that it doesn't require algebraic skills but is does require a bit of effort to learn. BUT IT'S SOOOOOOO FUN!

I included the Selling & Marketing section in this introduction to POD book because

1) I wanted to make sure you knew that this wasn't about creating 1 book or shirt and all your troubles were over. Sorry, it doesn't work that way. Businesses require work.
2) I wanted to include a video that shows you a little bit about doing keyword research on Amazon. Check it out!

Here's a video explaining how to research for Keywords on Amazon and will help in understanding Amazon's Best Seller's Rank (BSR).

Use the link below or scan the QR code with your smartphone camera.

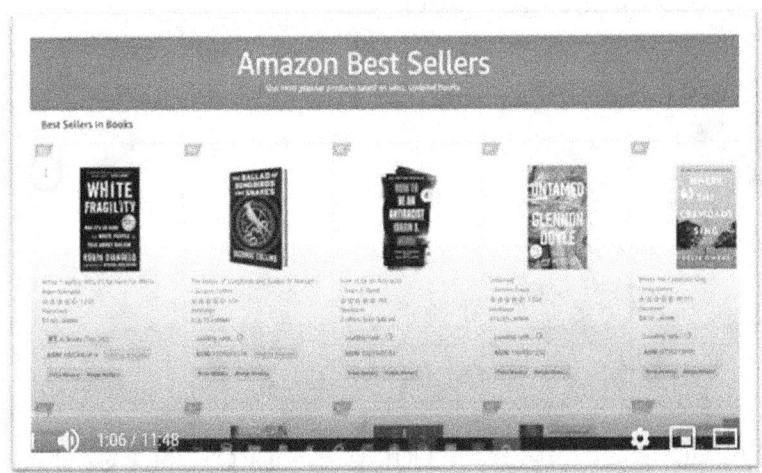 

https://youtu.be/2Kf6eRyjeyw

# Conclusion

Print of Demand is an amazing business! Especially for the mobile, always on the move military spouse. Believe me I know! I absolutely love the freedom and passive income this business has brought me. It is work, but it is a work I love and have a passion for.

If you are willing to learn, adjust as you learn, and be consistent in making and uploading products.... YOU WILL SUCCEED.

As a bonus, you can do this business in your spare time. Consistent effort will start and grow your business. You'll be amazed at how creating a book or two during your lunch hour every day will add up. Good luck in your journey in POD.

You don't have to do it all on your own! Check out the following pages on how I can help you continue to learn and succeed.

To sign up for my email list and 365+ Low Content Book ideas for free!

## www.ashschmitt.com

# Want this to be you? Want to Jumpstart your POD Business?

**COME CHECK OUT MY PUBLISHING BOOTCAMP FOR BEGINNERS.**

## YOU'LL LEARN

- HOW <u>EXACTLY</u> TO CREATE AMAZING LOW CONTENT BOOK INTERIORS THAT SELL
- HOW TO CREATE BOOK COVERS THAT STAND OUT
- A SYSTEM FOR STARTING YOUR PUBLISHING BUSINESS AND GROWING IT

## BONUSES INCLUDE

- A BEGINNER'S CHECKLIST
- INTERIOR AND COVER TEMPLATES
- QUICK REFERENCE SIZING CHARTS
- POWERPOINT SOFTWARE PROGRAM TO SPEED UP THE COVER MAKING PROCESS

<u>WWW.ASHSCHMITT.COM</u>

Want Weekly Tips & Tricks for Publishing Low Content Books?

Subscribe to my YouTube Channel

I am LIVE on Wednesdays at noon eastern time!

Use Link below or Scan the QR code with your smartphone.

https://www.youtube.com/channel/UCakY7BZO55bwY5znc28TnZw

www.ingramcontent.com/pod-product-compliance
Lightning Source LLC
Chambersburg PA
CBHW080446220526
45465CB00007B/2786